DID YOU HEAR THAT?

ANIMALS WITH SUPER HEARING

Caroline Arnold

Illustrated by **Cathy Trachok**

Charlesbridge

Published by Charlesbridge Publishing
85 Main Street, Watertown, MA 02472
(617) 926-0329
www.charlesbridge.com

Library of Congress Cataloging-in-Publication Data
Arnold, Caroline.
Did you hear that?: animals with super hearing/
Caroline Arnold; illustrations by Cathy Trachok.
p.   cm.
ISBN 1-57091-404-4 (reinforced for library use)
ISBN 1-57091-405-2 (softcover)
1. Sound production by animals—Juvenile Literature.
2. Hearing—Juvenile literature. [1. Animal sounds.
2. Sound.] I. Trachok, Cathy, ill. II. Title.
QL765.A75   2001
591.59'4—dc21   00-038369

Printed in the United States of America
(hc) 10 9 8 7 6 5 4 3 2 1
(sc) 10 9 8 7 6 5 4 3 2 1

Display type and text type set in Cheltenham, Eras, and Futura Condensed
Color separations by Eastern Rainbow, Derry, New Hampshire
Printed and bound by Phoenix Color, Rockaway, New Jersey
Production supervision by Brian G. Walker
Designed by Rosanne Kakos-Main

THE WORLD OF SOUND

Sixty years ago a scientist at Harvard University named Donald Griffin was studying bats. He watched them swoop and glide as they caught insects. Even though it was dark, the bats never bumped into anything. Griffin wanted to know why. He caught some bats and took them to another scientist who had invented a machine that could detect super high sounds. The bats seemed to be silent in their cage, but when the machine was turned on, it showed that the bats were actually making all sorts of noises. This was the first clue to understanding why bats are such expert fliers. Later research revealed that they use the echoes of these high-pitched sounds to "see" the night world.

We measure how high or low a sound is in hertz. The low bottom note on a piano is 30 hertz. The highest note is 4,100 hertz. People can hear sounds that are between 20 hertz and 20,000 hertz.

A Super Sense of Hearing

Most of the noises that bats make are above the range of human hearing. Many animals have the ability to detect sounds that we can't hear. Some, such as cats and dogs, can hear noises higher than a mouse's squeak. Others, such as elephants and some birds, can hear sounds lower than the rumble of distant thunder. All of these animals have a super sense of hearing. People can only detect these superhigh or superlow sounds with the help of special listening devices.

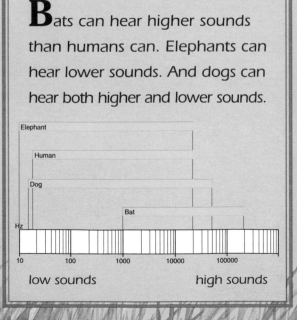

Bats can hear higher sounds than humans can. Elephants can hear lower sounds. And dogs can hear both higher and lower sounds.

Elephant	
Human	
Dog	
Bat	

Hz

10   100   1000   10000   100000

low sounds   high sounds

Opossums, guinea pigs, sloths, armadillos, anteaters, chinchillas, monkeys, and lemurs can hear ultrasounds too.

lemur

anteater

vervet monkey

armadillo

ABOVE THE RANGE
OF HUMAN HEARING

Have you ever seen a dog come running in answer to a "silent" whistle? The whistle is silent only to human ears. The dog can easily hear its extremely high pitched noises.

Sounds higher than 20,000 hertz are called ultrasounds. These sounds are made of many small, quick vibrations. We can't hear ultrasounds, but dogs, cats, bats, insects, dolphins, and hamsters can. Animals use ultrasounds to locate food, to find their way in the dark, and to communicate with each other.

Bats

Bats are the experts of the ultrasonic world. They are divided into two groups, the microbats and the megabats. Most microbats are insect eaters. All microbats rely on ultrasound to guide them when they fly and to help them find food and communicate with each other. The large, fruit-eating megabats can make ultrasounds too, but they do not use them when flying or searching for food. They can see well in dim light.

MEGABATS

Wahlberg's epauletted fruit bat

Red flying fox

Straw-colored fruit bat

Bats make sounds in their voice box just like you do. Some bats send out sounds through their mouths. Other bats use their noses. These bats often have flaps of skin on their faces called nose leaves. Scientists think that they may use these flaps to point the sound in a certain direction. Bats can direct their cries very precisely, in the same way that you can point a flashlight to shine a narrow beam of light.

Frog-eating fringe-lipped bat

MICROBATS

Australian ghost bat

Greater bulldog bat

Mexican free-tailed bat

A bat can easily fly through tangled branches or a narrow window opening because it "sees" the edges with sound.

Leaf-nosed bat

Bats "See" with Sound

Have you ever shouted into a cave and heard the echo of your voice? Bats use echoes to find their way in the dark. They send out streams of high-pitched sounds and listen for echoes bouncing off objects around them. It is like having a built-in radar system that uses sound instead of radio waves to "see" objects. This is called sonar. Sonar helps bats learn about the texture and shape of an object as well as its size and location. Sonar may even tell them which insects are good to eat and which are not.

When an animal uses sonar to get information about its environment, we say that it is echolocating. Microbats use ultrasounds to echolocate. One species of megabat uses clicks we can hear to find its way in caves.

Bats "Talk" with Ultrasound

Mother Mexican free-tailed bats often live in large caves with their babies. At night the mother bats leave the cave to catch insects to eat. When they return at dawn each mother searches for her own baby among the millions of baby bats. Each mother knows her own baby's ultrasonic cry. She calls out to her baby and listens for its answer. When she finds her baby she smells it to make sure that it is hers. Bats may also use ultrasounds to tell one another where there is a good place to find food.

Mexican free-tailed bats

Each kind, or species, of bat makes its own patterns of sounds. Scientists can recognize bats by their ultrasonic "voices."

Cricket

Owlet moth

One kind of owlet moth is called Heliothis zea. Its larva, the bollworm, eats growing corn, tomatoes, and cotton and is a serious pest for farmers.

Insects use a part of the body called the tympanic organ to detect sound vibrations in the air.

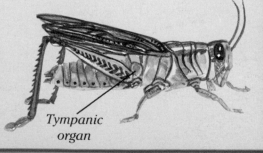

Tympanic organ

Bollworm

Insects

Owlet moths are common night-flying insects that are hunted by bats. An owlet moth's ability to hear ultrasounds helps it to know if bats are around. When a bat comes close, the moth veers out of the way and often avoids being caught.

Many insects make and hear ultrasounds. Some use the sounds to avoid predators or to stake a claim to their territory. Some sing ultrasonic "songs" to attract mates. Others make ultrasounds to warn other insects that danger is near.

Crickets, katydids, and cicadas make sounds by rapidly rubbing their front wings together. Other insects vibrate special membranes or squirt fluids from their bodies to make ultrasounds.

Cicada

Katydid

When a male rat starts a fight, he makes one kind of ultrasound. If he wants to stop the fight and retreat, he makes another kind of ultrasound.

Rats, Mice, and Other Rodents

A newborn hamster is blind, hairless, and helpless. If it wanders away from its nest and becomes lost, it makes special baby ultrasonic cries. When the mother hears them she finds the baby and brings it back to the nest.

Many rodents, including rats, mice, hamsters, and gerbils, can make and hear ultrasounds. They use them when mating, fighting, and defending their territory.

Most predators of rodents cannot hear ultrasounds unless they are very close. By using these almost silent sounds, rodents have a kind of secret language that allows them to "talk" to one another without being easily detected by other animals.

Tenrecs, Moles, and Other Insect Eaters

   Tenrecs are spiny animals that live on the island of Madagascar in the Indian Ocean. They go out at night to search for insects, worms, and plants to eat. When a tenrec rattles its spines, they make a clatter of ultrasonic noises. Then the other members of the group rush over to see what it has found.

   Tenrecs, moles, shrews, and hedgehogs are insect-eating mammals called insectivores. These animals are active mainly at night or underground. All of them can hear ultrasounds. Ultrasounds may help them find their way in the dark. They may also be useful for communicating with one another.

Tenrec

Hedgehog

Mole

Shrew

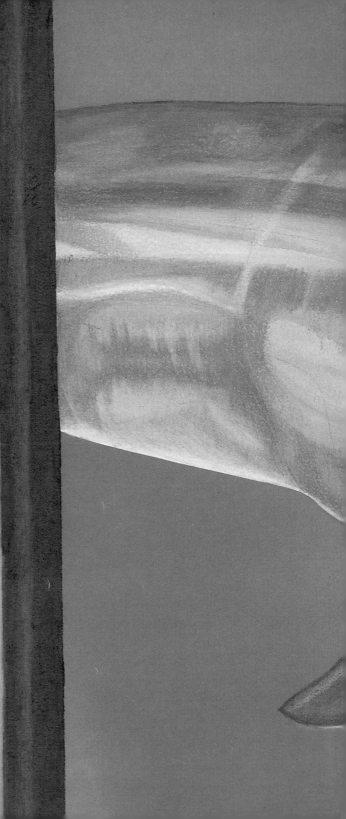

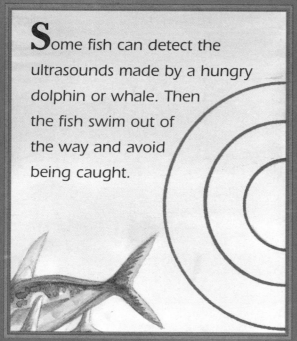

Some fish can detect the ultrasounds made by a hungry dolphin or whale. Then the fish swim out of the way and avoid being caught.

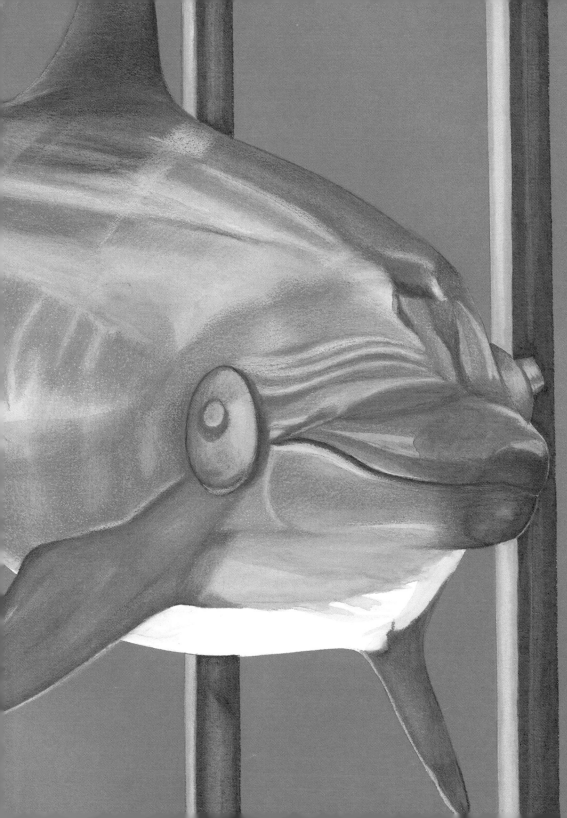

Ultrasounds in the Sea

Winthrop Kellogg was a scientist who trained bottlenose dolphins to go through an obstacle course of pipes. In one experiment he covered the dolphins' eyes. The dolphins went through the course again, and even though they couldn't see, they did it perfectly. They were "seeing" with sonar, much as bats do.

Dolphins are toothed whales. So are orcas, or killer whales. All of the toothed whales use sonar both to echolocate and to find food.

Sonar is a good way to find your way in the ocean. Even when the water is deep, dark, or cloudy, animals that can "see" with sound have no trouble finding their way.

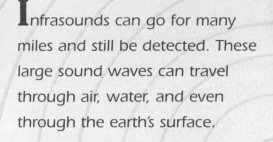

Infrasounds can go for many miles and still be detected. These large sound waves can travel through air, water, and even through the earth's surface.

BELOW THE RANGE OF HUMAN HEARING

Arctic terns are birds that migrate between Alaska and South America each year. As they fly they listen to the wind and the sounds of distant thunder. They may be able to use this information to avoid storms and choose the safest route when they travel.

Sounds lower than 20 hertz are infrasounds. Rumbling thunder, earthquake vibrations, and whirling tornadoes create infrasounds. The roar of wind as it passes over mountains or through canyons also produces infrasounds. Birds, fish, alligators, prairie dogs, and elephants are some of the animals that can hear these superlow sounds.

Elephants

Katy Payne is a scientist who was watching elephants one day at a zoo. She couldn't hear any elephant noises, but she sensed some low, rumbly vibrations. She came back later with a special tape recorder that could detect superlow sounds. She discovered that the elephants were making many noises—all below the range of human hearing. On the African plain, infrasounds help elephants stay in touch with others in their group even when they are too far apart to see or smell one another.

Elephants can say many things with infrasounds. They say "hello," tell each other where they are, and look for mates.

Rhinoceroses

One day scientists were watching elephants at a zoo and recording their infrasounds. Then they noticed that some of the sounds were coming from another animal enclosure nearby. Inside that enclosure were some rhinoceroses. The scientists discovered that rhinos are another animal that can make very low sounds. Like elephants, rhinos may use infrasounds to communicate with each other. Some other African animals that make superlow sounds are hippos, giraffes, lions, and okapis.

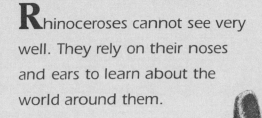

Rhinoceroses cannot see very well. They rely on their noses and ears to learn about the world around them.

Low Sounds in the Sea

A fish splashing in the water makes noises that include some very low sounds. A silky shark can hear these sounds up to a quarter of a mile away. Then it swims over to see if there might be something good to eat. Most sharks are good at detecting low sounds in the water. They use this information to find food.

Many ocean mammals, including whales and porpoises, have a good sense of hearing. Some can hear both very high and very low sounds. The common porpoise uses the echoes of very low sounds to find its way around the ocean. Humpback whales may use very low sounds to communicate with each other over distances of more than one hundred miles.

Silver-tip shark

Water is a good conductor of sound. Sound travels much farther and faster in water than it does in air.

A SUPER SENSE OF HEARING

The natural world is filled with sounds. Thunder claps, waves crash, and leaves rustle. Dogs bark, birds sing, and crickets chirp. Sounds tell us about the weather, our surroundings, and who is nearby.

To us our surroundings often seem noisy. But for some animals the world is a very different place. Many animals—from bats and dolphins to elephants and rhinoceroses—are able to make and hear extremely high or extremely low sounds. They have a super sense of hearing that helps them to survive. We can only imagine what it might be like to live in their squeaky and rumbly world.

WEB RESOURCES

"BCI's Bat Chat Audiotape."
Bat Conservation International.
http://www.batcon.org/discover/echo.html
- Hear audio samples of bat ultrasounds.

Fauna Communications Research Institute.
http://www.animalvoice.com/Links.htm
- A good links list. General information about animal communications can be found elsewhere on the site.

"Long Distance Elephant Communication."
Pittsburgh Zoo.
http://zoo.pgh.pa.us/elephant communication.html
- A good source for learning about elephant infrasound research.

Whale Acoustics Project.
http://newport.pmel.noaa.gov/whales/whale-calls.html
- Hear recordings of whale sounds, speeded up so humans can hear them.

GLOSSARY

echolocation—a way of locating objects through the use of echoes

hertz—the unit used for measuring the highness, or pitch, of a sound

infrasound—a sound below the range of human hearing; less than 20 hertz

insectivores—insect-eating mammals

mammals—animals that give birth to live young and nourish their young with milk from the mother's body

megabats—the large, fruit-eating bats of the Tropics

microbat—the majority of bats worldwide; most are small and are insect eaters.

rodents—gnawing mammals

ultrasound—a sound above the range of human hearing; more than 20,000 hertz